KHALED BOUKEBBOUS

SUSTAINABLE NEURO-CHEMICAL ALTERATION© (SNCA)

A new approach to positive change

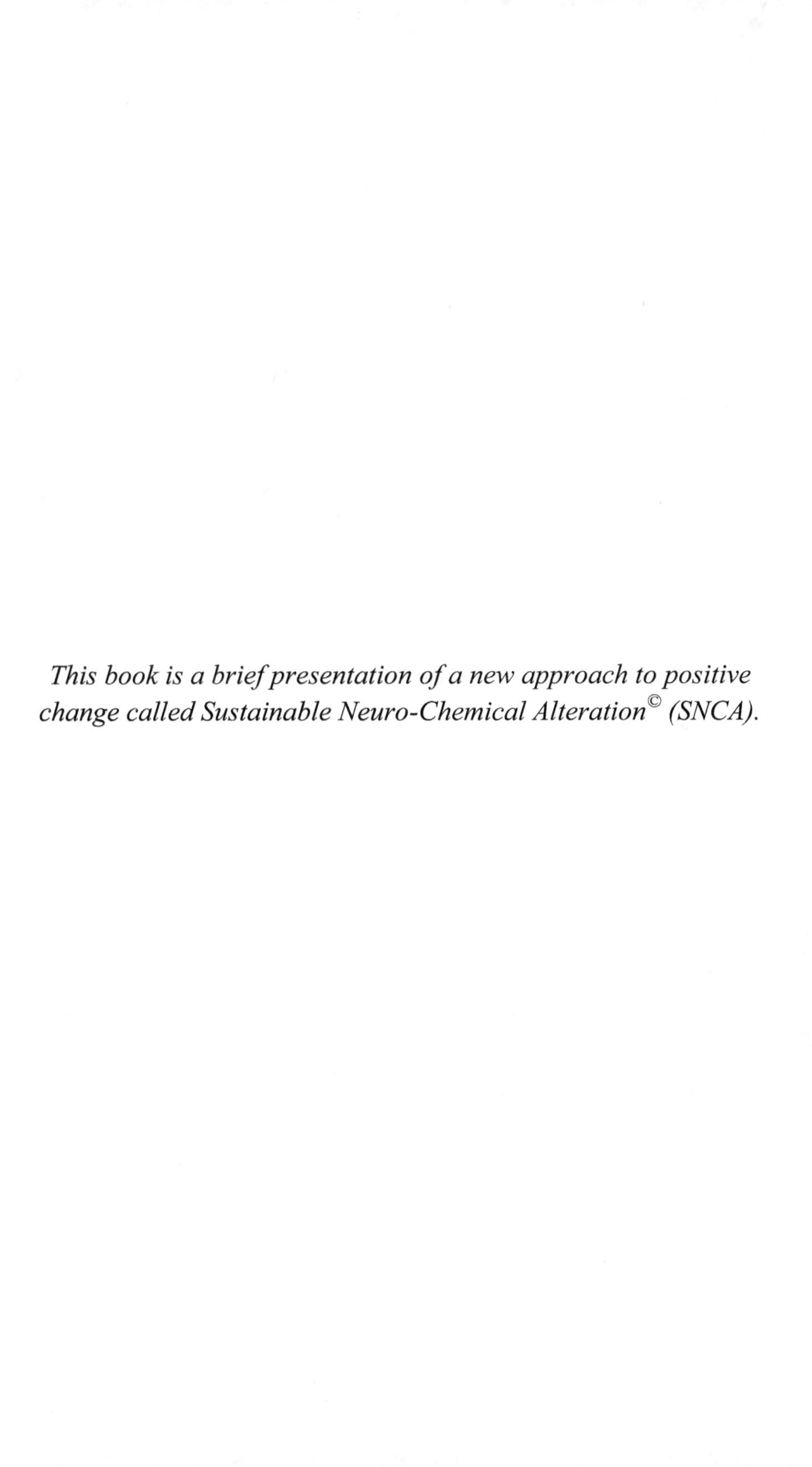

This book is a brief presentation of a new approach to positive change called Sustainable Neuro-Chemical Alteration[©] (SNCA).

I dedicate this book

To my parents, modest people with unlimited generosity,

To my family,

To all those who want to make a positive change in this world.

Dr. Khaled Boukebbous, the SNCA approach creator.

I have spent the last years of my life for understanding the interaction between the mind and body, also between the mind and reality.

The number of scientific studies that I have found talking about these interactions directly or indirectly was unbelievable. Unfortunately, almost only specialized scientists read these kinds of scientific studies, which means that the majority of people stay ignoring totally the existence of very helpful and empowering knowledge.

So rapidly, I have understood that I must simplify and summarize this empowering knowledge then spread it to the large people because I sincerely believe that this knowledge can make a shift in the global consciousness and enhance the lives of many people on this planet. The simplification of the recent scientific facts gives a born to a new approach to positive change that I call it: the SNCA approach.

CONTENT

INTRODUCTION

*"You never change things by fighting the existing reality.
To change something, build a new model that makes the existing
model obsolete."*

Richard Buckminster Fuller

When we look at the recent scientific researches made over the last two decades, we can clearly observe that there is a substantial amount of scientific studies that demonstrate how our minds have an incredible creative power that affects every side of our lives. These researches and studies both reported and highlighted a considerable quantity of empowering information that could lead to a fabulous transformation of our lives and a significant improvement in this world. Unfortunately, the existence of the kind of helpful information is unknown to most people.

Thousands of recent studies in many scientific fields demonstrate that the mind impacts each dimension of life, where a strong connection between the state of mind and the state of the body is established; likewise, a robust interaction between the perceptions and the living reality is also verified.

This book introduces a new approach to positive change and evolutions that can fabulously transform individuals' lives. It also brings together many principles, ideas, and scientific facts in a very simple way in order to help as many people as possible to restructure their existence.

The empowering beliefs of this approach can help people to be more aware of the events of their own life and are also an outlet to those who also feel the strong desire to free themselves from the prison of the prevailing norms.

THE ORIGIN OF SNCA

The mind-body and mind-reality interactions are constantly shaping our lives in an incredible way; unfortunately, the majority of people little knows or ignores the existence of these kinds of interactions completely.

My research to understand the mind-body and the mind-reality interactions, conduct me to a very simple result. I have found that the basis of change is an alteration in the brain activity (how neurons fire and wire together) accompanied by a modification in the chemical balance (the level of chemicals released in the brain and body). As a result, I have found that the substantial root of any permanent change is a sustainable alteration in our neurocircuitry and sustainable modification in our chemical balance. Accordingly, I can define permanent change as a Sustainable Neuro-Chemical Alteration (SNCA).

Knowing that the mindset and the emotional state are directly related to the brain activities and the chemical balance, respectively, we can say as well that the permanent change is a sustainable modification in the mindset and the emotional state.

The SNCA approach focuses on the real changes in the brain and body and their relation with the changes in the mindset and the emotional state.

The SNCA approach also concentrates on the understanding of the inner world (what is going on in our minds, brains, and bodies) and its influence on the outer world (states of being, actions, behaviors, outcomes).

WHAT IS SNCA IN SHORT WORDS?

SNCA represents a new approach to positive change and self-development based on scientific facts that can be used by coaches and therapists in their practices or by any other people looking for improving their lives. The SNCA approach contains twelve central beliefs (principles) founded on the most fabulous and powerful scientific studies. Besides, the SNCA approach divides the life domains into four main domains rather than eight, as commonly known.

THE MAIN BELIEFS OR PRINCIPLES OF THE SNCA

There are twelve central beliefs or principles suggested by the SNCA approach. The results of recent scientific studies support these twelve principals; these lasts can make significant changes in your way of thinking and wonderfully transform your life. So, let's go through these twelve principals one by one.

THE FIRST PRINCIPLE

The brain is a dynamic organ that changes and adapts all the time

A large part of people still thinking that our brains are unchangeable in adulthood. But in fact, our brains regularly change throughout our lives span according to our way of thinking, feeling, and behaving. Furthermore, every skill we acquire or every experience we went through as well as every piece of information we learn, can modify our brains in different ways (chemically, structurally, and functionally); this phenomenon is called brain plasticity or neuroplasticity. The plasticity in our brains is an ordinary mechanism that allows us to learn, change, develop, and grow in our lives. Neuroplasticity can be negative and generates many issues in our brains, then causes considerable problems in our lives; also, neuroplasticity can be positive and supports the good functioning of our brains then produces significant improvements in our lives. The brain is the most dominating organ in the body, and any change occurring in it will influence the whole body and the entire life. So, changes in our lives are actually engendered by changes in our brains.

Researchers in neuroscience[1] discovered that the adult male human brain contains on average 86.1 billion neurons and 84.6 billion non-neuronal cells called glial cells. 19% of all neurons and 72% of all the glial cells are located in the cerebral cortex, which represents 82% of total brain mass. Besides, 80% of all neurons and 19% of all the glial cells are located in the cerebellum, which represents 10% of the whole brain mass. The rest 1% of neurons and 9% of glial cells are located in the limbic brain, which represents 8% of total brain mass.

Each neuron can form thousands of links within other neurons; these links are called synaptic connections, where the region of interaction between two neurons is named synapse. The average number of synaptic connections in the human brain is estimated by one thousand trillion (10^{15}). Once these connections are established, the information passing through them is assured by electrical signals called an action potential, and chemical signals called neurotransmitters. The synaptic connections are involved in all brain activities, such as learning, memory, language, emotions, thinking, etc. The connections between neurons change continuously during our lifespan. Every time we learn something new, practice new skills, go through new experiences, new synaptic connections are made, and become stronger as long as the same connections are used.

---

[1] *Azevedo FA, et al; Equal numbers of neuronal and nonneuronal cells make the human brain an isometrically scaled-up primate brain; The Journal of Comparative Neurology; 2009 Apr 10;513(5):532-41.*

THE SECOND PRINCIPLE

The mindset and the state of being are closely associated

Every thought crosses our minds makes tiny changes in our brains and small modifications in our bodies. Whereas a persistent thought makes significant and lasting changes in our brains (creating new and strong synaptic connections, also activating or deactivating different neurocircuitries). Moreover, a persistent thought makes substantial modifications in our bodies (lasting chemical and biological alterations), which directly impacts our state of being. Therefore, thinking in the same way for an extended period of time makes substantial and lasting changes in the brain and body that can be positive or negative according to the quality of our thoughts. As a result, when we change our way of thinking (mindset), we change our state of being (health condition). So, both negative and positive thoughts can modify the chemistry of our bodies, such as hormones and neurotransmitters, which can impact the functioning of every cell of our bodies and make them live under adverse conditions or favorable conditions, which affects our health negatively or positively.

Most people do not realize that their mindsets inluence the quality of their lives, and even worse, they entirely ignore that their mindsets are directly affecting their health. The positive mindset can make us avoid several problems such as stress and anxiety that are related in the long-term to enormous and severe health problems, such as sleep disorders, rheumatism, cardiovascular issues, urticaria, eczema, depression, neurodegenerative diseases, diabetes, and even cancer. Besides, the positive mindset generates vital energy that reinforces our immune defenses and helps for the excellent functioning of every cell in our bodies, which keeps us in good health and a positive state of being.

On the other hand, the negative mindset can kill us in the proper sense of the word. It weakens our immune systems, absorbs our energy, disturbs the functioning of every cell in our bodies, and significantly increases the number of health issues.

A study made by Yale University and Arizona State University demonstrates that the mindset influences the level of hormones in the body[1]. In this study, researchers endeavored to study the impact of the mindset on a precise hormone called ghrelin hormone or hunger hormone, knowing that a high level of ghrelin translated to a feeling of hunger and a need to eat; whereas, the low level of ghrelin implies that we are full, and we do not need to eat.

On two separate occasions, 46 participants consumed a 380-calorie milkshake, but on the first occasion, researchers pretended that they had given them a 140-calorie shake instead; on the second occasion, researchers pretended that they had given them a 620-calorie milkshake. Ghrelin was measured via intravenous blood samples at three time points: baseline (20 min), anticipatory (60 min), and post-consumption (90 min). The result was fascinating. On the occasion where the participants thought that they were consuming a 140-calorie shake, the measures showed that the level

---

[1] *Alia J. Crum, et al; Mind Over Milkshakes: Mindsets, Not Just Nutrients, Determine Ghrelin Response; Health Psychology; 2011, Vol. 30, No. 4, 424 – 429.*

of the ghrelin hormone did not show a substantial decrease, which meant that the participants felt hungry, and their bodies wanted more food. However, on the occasion where the participants thought that they were consuming a 620-calorie milkshake, the measures showed that the level of ghrelin hormone decreased significantly, which meant that participants felt full and their bodies did not want more food. The result of this study demonstrates and highlights that the mindset affects the body's chemical balance. So, the chemical balance in our brains and bodies is directly affected by the mindset and that whatever the reality is.

Till now, we have understood that the mindset directly affects our chemical balance? But why the chemical balance is too important for us?

There are trillions of cells in the human body, and there are over 100000 chemical reactions occur per and second per cell.

The change in the mindset leads to a change in the chemical balance, which influences the chemical reactions occurring in each cell and the performance of every organ in our bodies.

The positive mindset translates to favorable chemical balance in the brain and body, then this favorable chemical balance supports neurogenesis and cells repair, supports a high level of energy, promotes for favorable genes expressions, supports the good food digestion and storage, supports the toxins elimination process, helps for getting robust immune defenses, promotes for a healthy cardiovascular system, and as we know the favorable chemical balance translates to positive emotional state, which means positive emotions and feelings. Unfortunately, the opposite is also true.

The negative mindset translates to unfavorable chemical balance in the brain and body, then this unfavorable chemical balance obstructs neurogenesis and cells repair, obstructs high level of energy, conducts to unfavorable genes expressions, obstructs the good food digestion and storage, obstructs the toxins elimination process, conducts to a weak immune system, causes many issues in the cardiovascular system, and as we know the unfavorable chemical balance translates to negative emotional state, which means negative emotions and feelings.

An international study made by Harvard University and other institutes in Italy found that the mindset has an incredible effect on our health and wellbeing[1].

This study was conducted in six days on a group of older adults, where researchers made them envision themselves living in time going back twenty years in the past. By the end of this study, the participants found improvement in hearing, enhancement in memory, improvement in muscle strength, improvement in vision, amelioration in joint flexibility, increase in manual skills, increase in mental abilities, enhancement in posture and gait, decrease in symptoms of arthritis, and even they look significantly younger. But what happened there? When participants began to imagine themselves living in a time that dates back twenty years in the past, they started positively changing their self-images, their thinking, their inner dialogues, their beliefs about their abilities, and their expectations; in other words, they began to adapt younger and more favorable mindset. This positive mindset translated to favorable chemical balance, and this favorable chemical balance impacted the functioning of every organ and every cell in their bodies, which turned to many improvements in their health and wellbeing.

In another study conducted over six years in Germany, the researchers found that people who had a positive perception of themselves and their old age had much better health than those who had

---

[1] *Pagnini F, et al. BMJ Open 2019;9:e030411.*

a negative perception.

In short words, you have to make close attention to your mind-set because it enormously impacts your state of being where the positive mindset promotes health and wellbeing. Whereas, the negative mindset causes illness and diseases.

So, keep this in your mind: *the mindset and the state of being are closely associated,* and never forget that your state of being is also crucial for having high performance and succeeding in anything you undertake in this life.

THE THIRD PRINCIPLE

The change in the mindset translates to tangible changes in life

When our minds begin to be shaped by a new idea, physical changes in our brains and bodies begin to occur. Therefore, once the mind starts to be positively shaped by ambitious goals, a big mission, or a new and better vision of the future, the chemistry, the biology, and the energy of the whole body begin to be positively shaped as well, according to these goals, mission, or vision. After a while, remarkable and lasting changes start to appear on all sides of our existence and in the outcomes of anything we undertake. Unfortunately, when our minds begin to be shaped by negative ideas, adverse outcomes begin to manifest in our lives too. As a result, to make a positive change or to create a better life, we need to reshape our minds by new ideas about a better future rather than keep thinking about the bad past and the previous negative experiences.

In fact, the big goals, the ambitious visions, and the inspiring missions have much more power to mobilize your potential and to improve your performance than moderately tricky goals, vision or mission can do.

A study carried out at Bishop's University demonstrates that just thinking and doing mental training on its own can produce tangible changes in our bodies[1].

For three weeks, thirty male university athletes participated in this study. The first ten were randomly allocated to a mental training group that mentally practiced hip flexions. The second ten participants were assigned to a physical training group that exercised using a hip flexor weight machine. The third ten participants formed a control group that had neither been given mental nor physical training.

The result was astonishing when the control group, that hadn't done anything in particular, saw no gains in strength. The exercise group that had been training three times a week saw a 28% gain in strength, no big surprises there! But the group that did not exercise, but thought about exercising instead, experienced nearly as the same gains in strength as the exercise group where this group had on average, 24% gain in strength. This was a very astonishing result.

In addition, mental and physical training produced similar decreases in heart rate, and both groups yielded a marginal reduction in systolic blood pressure.

A similar study published in Neuropsychologia journal[2] – which targets another body muscle – conducted to comparable results, while mental training showed strengthening by 35%, the physical training showed strengthening by 53%.

---

[1] *Erin M. Shackell and Lionel G. Standing; Mind Over Matter: Mental Training Increases Physical Strength; North American Journal of Psychology, 2007, Vol. 9, No. 1 189-200.*

[2] *Vinoth K.Ranganathan, et al; From mental power to muscle power—gaining strength by using the mind; Neuropsychologia; 42, 944–956 (2004).*

But what happened there?

When the participants began to think and visualize themselves practicing a precise exercise, the created thoughts and self-images in their minds began to make chemical and biological changes, then these chemical and biological changes manifested tangibly in their bodies and that in coherence with the created thoughts and self-images in their minds.

Put this in your mind: your mindset is the most powerful tool of creation in the universe. Think continually about something, and an equivalent reality will manifest in your life.

Many people thought that thinking about a better future is a refuge from the real world to an imaginary world. In fact, thinking about a better future doesn't mean refuge in an imaginary world that can never be real.

The scientific studies show that thinking about a better future and having a clear vision change your life now in the present because when you start thinking about a better future, you begin immediately impacting your chemical balance and causing biological modifications. These last drive tangible and positive changes. So when you start reshaping your mind by great ideas such as big goals, ambitious vision, exciting mission, and powerful self-image, you do not refuge in an imaginary world, but, in fact, you begin creating a new and better life.

So, put this in your mind, when you start thinking about a better life and create a better self-image in your mind, you begin tangibly improving your life. And never forget that *the change in the mindset translates to tangible changes in life.*

THE FOURTH PRINCIPLE

*The mindset and the chemical balance
are the two main components
of everyone's identity*

Thought in our minds is a neural activity in our brains that influences the trigger of specific chemicals in the brain and body, which causes the feelings and emotions that drive decisions and actions. How we think, how we feel, how we decide, and how we behave represent the fundamentals of our personality and our identity. Therefore, the mindset and the chemical balance structure who we are, which means a lasting change in these two last, leads to a change in our personality. As a result, we cannot create new personal reality as the same personality; we need to change our personality, which means becoming someone different and better than the old version of ourselves. So, when we change our mindset and our chemical balance, we change our nature and personality; and when we change our nature and personality, we change our reality.

Many people spend a large part of their lives with negative mindsets and unfavorable emotional states that push them to make wrong decisions and take bad actions. Then they usually wonder why they are getting poor outcomes repeatedly.

When they think negatively and engender unhelpful feelings and emotions such as anger, frustration, depression, and shame, their decisions and actions become destructive with which they cannot grow, evolve, and make positive changes.

Moreover, the negative results of their bad decisions and actions approve the same negative mindsets and emphasize the same unfavorable emotional states; this makes them stuck in the same negative situations for a long time and maybe eternally.

In opposite, happy, healthy, wealthy, and successful people focus on maintaining a positive mindset and favorable emotional state to ensure making good decisions and taking the right actions that enable them to get the results that they want. Then the positive outcomes of their good decisions and actions support the same positive mindsets and emphasize the same favorable emotional states; this makes them flourish, evolve, and grow in their lives continually.

So, we know that our mindsets generate our emotions, and we know that any decision we make in our lives, we take it based on our way of thinking and on our way of feeling. Negative Emotions like acute stress or anger are the worst emotions to make decisions or to take action. They are related to selfish, rude, and aggressive personality. Moreover, negative emotions like shame, guilt, and depression can make us unable to make good decisions and take the right actions. These emotions are related to confused, closed, inactive, and submissive personality.

On the other hand, positive emotions like love, enthusiasm, and passion, are very helpful for taking action. They Are related to enthusiastic, energetic, and persisting personality. Moreover, emotions like admiration, relaxation, gratitude, appreciation, recognition, and fullness are great to make decisions. They appear in our lives as a generous, helpful, wise, confident, and self-esteemed personality.

So, put this in your mind, you can't create a better life as the same personality; you have to become someone different and better than your old personality. And that by changing your mindset and your emotional state positively and permanently.

How can a change in the mindset become a change in personality?

We know that the adoption of new ideas and the changes in the mindset drive changes in the chemical balance, which in turn translate to feelings and emotions; these feelings and emotions in their turn influence decisions, actions, and behavior. All these changes show up as changes in the mood.

When you maintain these changes in the mindset for an extended period of time, they become beliefs and automatic programs in your mind. Also, when you retain the new chemical balance and the new engendered emotions and feelings for an extended period of time, they become chemical addictions and biological alterations in your brain and body. Besides, when you keep the new way of deciding, acting, and behaving for a long time, it becomes habits, routines, and rituals in your life. All these changes show up as changes in character, identity, and personality.

As a result, the negative change in the mindset, after a certain time, becomes a negative and weak personality.

However, the positive change in the mindset, after a certain time, becomes a positive and powerful personality.

So, put this in your mind, you can change your personality to become what you want to be. And never forget that what is turning on in your mind is reshaping your personality and identity.

THE FIFTH PRINCIPLE

The perception of the outer world reflects the state of the inner world

As long as we have the same mindset and the same chemical balance, we keep feeling, deciding, and acting in the same way, then getting the same outcomes and living the same life. When we change our mindset and our chemical balance, we change our way of feeling and behaving; subsequently, we start getting different outcomes and living a different life, which changes our perception of the world entirely. Therefore, the change in the mindset induces plasticity in the brain, modifies the chemical balance, alters the state of being, modulates the personality, and then shapes the reality, which changes the perception of the whole world. As a result, how we see the world does not represent the reality of the world, but it reflects the reality of our inner world. So, each person in this life has a different perception of the world that depends fundamentally on his/her mindset and chemical balance.

So, put this in your mind, when you change your mindset and chemical balance, you change your inner world. And when you changer your inner world, you change your perception of the outer world.

We have to understand that our reality is always in harmony with our inner world because we cannot perceive a new reality if our mindset is not adapted to perceive it, we perceive only the reality that is in harmony with our mindset. At the same time, we think that it is the only reality that we can have in our lives. The other possible realities are not existing for us because we are not able to perceive them. So, to perceive new options for our lives, we need to change our inner world. A negative mindset and emotional state give a negative and limited perception of the world. Yet, a positive mindset and emotional state provide a positive and empowering perception of the world.

So, please put this in your mind, how you see the world reflect the quality of your mindset and emotional state and not the reality itself. And never forget that you can only get the reality that is in harmony with your mindset and emotional state.

THE SIXTH PRINCIPLE

The obstacles in people's lives lie basically in their minds

Beliefs represent the frames that define what we can do or not, what it is possible for us or not, what we deserve to have or not, and what we can be or not. We live in this world according to what we believe in our potentials, on our abilities, and our limits. When we believe that something can affect our lives in a particular way and expect that, our minds, brains, and bodies rearrange themselves chemically and biologically to make that happen, which conducts us to get precise outcomes that correspond to our beliefs and expectations. A change in the beliefs and expectations makes considerable changes in the lives of people. Therefore, once we get rid of limiting beliefs and adopt new empowering beliefs, we start discovering new potentials and possibilities in our lives that lead to transforming our existence magnificently. As a result, beliefs shape our entire existence and can hold us back or launch our potential.

I want to tell you a story:

Before 6th May, 1954, everyone thought that running a mile in less than 4 minutes was just impossible because it exceeded the limit of the human body. Of course, there was a whole environment that supported this belief, especially the sports' experts of that time who had declared that the human body simply was not capable of it. This belief has remained a firm conviction for several decades, and no one had ventured to break the boundaries of this limiting belief. Yet, on the 6th May, 1954, Rodger Bannister crushed this belief by running the one mile in front of everyone within three minutes and fifty-nine seconds. That day, Bannister put an end to a limiting belief in people's minds, and the "one mile in less than four minutes" became possible. A short time later, several athletes ran the "one mile in less than 4 minutes," and today, thousands of athletes do, including high school students.

So, put this in your mind, People who defeat the general mentality and the common beliefs are mainly people who make new possibilities in this world since every defeated limiting belief reveals new potentials for each individual and new horizons for humanity.

How beliefs influence our reality?

We think that we believe in what we see and experience in this life; in other words, our beliefs are the logical result of our reality. However, the truth is far from being the only case. The major part of what we see and experience in this life is what we believe; in short, our reality is the logical result of our beliefs. This truth is the key to bringing positive changes and significant improvements in our lives because changing a belief leads directly to changing the corresponding reality. Consequently, the power of beliefs resides in the ability to filtrate the truth and show us only the matching part with them, which becomes our personal reality.

Indeed, according to the quality of your mindset, notably your beliefs and expectations, you select the corresponding possibilities from an infinite number of options. So, if you have negative and limiting beliefs, you select bad possibilities, limited potential, and fixed meaning to be your personal reality. However, if you have positive and empowering beliefs, you select amazing possibilities, great potentials, and different meanings to be your personal reality. So, when you change your beliefs, you choose a new possible reality to become your personal reality.

So, put this in your mind, What holds you back in your life exist only in your mind, so when you change your mindset, you liberate yourself from your invisible chains, which allows you to unleash your true potential and to create a better life.

How far can a change in beliefs impact our lives?

A study carried out at Harvard University showed that beliefs could impact our lives and the outcomes of anything we undertake[1].

Eighty-four women who work as hotel housekeepers in seven different hotels participated in this study; these women are obliged to make a lot of effort every day because of the nature of their job. However, they don't see all these efforts as an exercise since the two-thirds of them confirm that they don't exercise regularly, and a third of them confirm that they don't exercise at all.

The researchers measured systolic blood pressure, body fat, and weight. Then they took half of these women and showed them a short presentation of 15 minutes to demonstrate them that their job was good in terms of exercise and satisfies the Surgeon General's recommendations for an active lifestyle so that they can consider their job as exercises and they have to obtain the same benefits as exercising. The second half of these women did not see any presentation. After four weeks, researchers made the same measurements again as before. The result of the half who they did not see the presentation hadn't shown any change. However, the result was astonishing for the group of women that had been shown the

---

[1] *Crum, Alia J., and Ellen J. Langer. 2007. Mind-set matters: Exercise and the placebo effect. Psychological Science 18, no. 2: 165-171.*

presentation since they had the same benefit of exercising, such as a loss of weight, a significant reduction in the systolic blood pressure, and a decrease in body fat.

But what happened there?

When the participants in the study started to believe that their daily efforts can be considered as exercises and began to expect the same effects of exercising, their brains and bodies rearrange themselves chemically and biologically to make that happen, which led them to get tangibly the same benefit of exercising. However, the participants who hadn't any change in their beliefs did not get any benefits from their daily effort despite the fact that they spent the same efforts as the participants who they got substantial changes in their bodies.

So, put this in your mind, a change in your beliefs leads to substantial changes in your life. And never forget that your mindset matter for the outcomes of anything you undertake in your life.

THE SEVENTH PRINCIPLE

People condition and recondition their brains and bodies repeatedly

Throughout our lives span, we have been intentionally or unintentionally changing our brains and bodies positively or negatively. When we repeat a new idea continually then feel it intensely, we will condition our brains and bodies chemically and biologically, which means that the new repeated idea becomes a conviction that remodels our lives positively or negatively. Also, when we receive an idea and take it directly as a fact, the taken idea can recondition our brains and bodies according to it. Furthermore, when we pass through special experiences in our lives then we stick with the same way of thinking and feeling that we have had in those special moments, we condition ourselves to live those experiences for the rest of our lives by making lasting changes in our minds, brains, and bodies. The conditioning permit to the particular idea or experience makes strong neuro-connections in our brains and familiar chemical balance in our bodies, which allow to this idea or experience to become natural, habitual, and logical for us.

Here is a little story of a man who in passing one day by a camp of elephants, noticed that all the elephants were neither kept in cages nor held by solid metal chains but only tied with a rope to one of their legs!

The man was unable to find a logical explanation for why these elephants had accepted to have this miserable life while they could have easily escaped and roamed freely in the beautiful forest.

To put an end to all his interrogations and confusions, the man approached the elephant trainer and said to him: I cannot understand how it is possible to put in captivity very powerful animals like these elephants only by using a simple rope? The elephant trainer answered him: when they were very young and small, they were much less powerful; so we only used these ropes to tie them up, and that was enough to keep them. They had tried to flee, but without succeeding, which conditioned them on the impossibility of escaping.

Growing up, they continued to believe that they could not flee and that the same ropes could still hold them; and have therefore never tried to free themselves, while they can do it easily with their present power. This was a very telling story because, unfortunately, most people on this planet have this kind of conditioning in their minds that prevents them from unleashing their true potentials and creating better lives.

When we maintain the same mindset for an extended period of time and keep repeatedly thinking in the same manner, we make new and strong neural connections, and we activate the same neurocircuits that become more and more dominating with every repetition, which means we condition ourselves neurologically to live the same experiences over and over again.

Also, When we maintain the same emotional state for a long time, we become addicted to precise chemical balance, which means we condition ourselves chemically to live the same experiences over and over again.

As well, when we decide, behave, and keep living in the same manner for an extended period of time, we make physical modifications in our bodies, and we generate alterations in our genes expressions, which means we condition ourselves biologically to live the same experiences and the same life over and over again.

So, when you want to condition yourself to be someone different that you have never been and to create a new life that you have never lived, you need to maintain your mindset, emotional state, and way of living in harmony with what you want until you condition your mind, brain, and body with it.

As a result, you have to make close attention to your repeated way of thinking, feeling, and behaving because it can condition you according to its nature. If this way of thinking, feeling, and behaving is positive, you condition yourself positively, but if it is negative, you condition yourself negatively.

THE EIGHTH PRINCIPLE

Making a permanent change is to reprogram the subconscious mind

Any lasting change in the body and life must have roots in the subconscious mind because we are operating a large part of our lives automatically from it. Once we have reprogrammed our subconscious minds as we want, change becomes an automatic process. When we change our minds consciously and durably, we change our brains physically and permanently; and when we change our brains permanently, we change our subconscious minds (reprogram the subconscious mind), which produces permanent changes in every dimension of our lives. So the mental changes have to be translated into lasting physical changes in our brains to become automatic programs that shape our lives, which means, to make a permanent change in the subconscious mind, we need to make a lasting change in the brain.

There are two parts of the mind. The first one is the conscious mind, which is the thinking strategies and thoughts that we are aware of, and that results in conscious decisions and behaviors, which through them, we influence our lives purposely. The second one is the subconscious mind, which is the thinking strategies and beliefs that influence our decisions and behaviors unconsciously, then impact our entire lives unintentionally.

Researchers revealed that we live a large part of our lives in an unconscious way[1]. They estimate that by the age of 35, more than 95 percent of our cognitive activities in this life are controlled by the unconscious and the automatic brain activities, and less than 5 percent of our cognitive activities are related to conscious and intentional brain activities. In other words, more than 95 percent of our thoughts, decisions, actions, emotions, behaviors, and outcomes are molded by automatic running programs we have had installed throughout our lives.

The subconscious mind has a phenomenal power; it has the capacity to process millions of bits of information (nerve impulses) per second. The Subconscious mind controls our habits, routines, skills, beliefs, as well the automatic ways of thinking, feeling, and reacting.

The conscious mind can only process a small number of bits of information (nerve impulses) per second, which means it is decidedly slower than the subconscious mind; however, its power resides in its creativity and its ability to reprogram the subconscious mind as we want.

The relationship between the conscious and subconscious mind is crucial to understand the mechanism of change and also the main obstacles to change.

When we repeat something for a long time, we go from intentional brain activity to an automatic brain activity that keeps working throughout our lifespan, from the past to the present, and maybe to the future if we don't intervene purposely to stop this

---

[1] *US News & World Report presented a special issue February 28, 2005, entitled, The Secret Mind, featuring and article, How Your Unconscious Really Shapes Your Decisions.*

automatic program. So, the change obliges to modify the automatic programs that the subconscious mind keeps running continually.

If we want to describe the relationship between the conscious and subconscious mind in one word, it will be repetition. Repetition permits to create strong neural connections in the brain that dominate the brain activity, which makes them automatic processes or programs. Therefore, the key to reprogramming our subconscious mind is conscious repetition.

So, if you want to change your life and to unleash your true potential, you should repeat what you want in a conscious way until it becomes a subconscious process and automatic program.

And remember that your subconscious controls more than 95% of your life. That means nothing is going to be changed if you don't change your subconscious mind.

THE NINTH PRINCIPLE

The inherited habits are vital as the inherited DNA

The habitual way of thinking, feeling, and behaving can regulate our gene expressions, which means that our habits can improve or deteriorate our health state. Having the same habits as our family or our environment could lead us to have the same health condition since the same habits cause the same regulation of gene expression. What does that mean? The inherited habits of thinking, feeling, and behaving are important as the inherited DNA from the parents, and they play a capital role in our health states. Accordingly, it is not only our DNA that determines our health states[1], but also our habits that can change the expression of our genes and recondition our brains and bodies in a good or bad way. Therefore, the development of good habits promotes a healthy, prosperous, and satisfying life. How we think, how we feel, and how we behave can regulate our gene expressions and affect our health, energy, performance, and outcomes positively or negatively. So, habits

---

[1] *Church, D. (2010). Your DNA is not your destiny: Behavioral epigenetics and the role of emotions in health. In R. Klatz & R. Goldman (Eds.), Anti-aging therapeutics (Vol. 13, pp. 35–42). Chicago, IL: A4M (American Academy of Anti-Aging Medicine).*

and genes both control our biology.

It has been identified that several lifestyle factors such as diet, obesity, physical activity, tobacco smoking, alcohol consumption, environmental pollutants, psychological stress, and working on night shifts might influence gene expression and cause epigenetic modifications[1]. What does that mean? That means eating healthy food or not, exercising your body or not, smoking or not, drinking alcohol or not, choosing to stay in a clean environment or not, feeling stressed of not, sleeping early and enough or not, have an impact on the expression of your gene. In short, your lifestyle or your habitual way of living affects your biology.

But why the lifestyle influence the gene expression?

The lifestyle factors change our chemical balance by adding or changing the level of many chemicals in our brains and bodies, such as melatonin, cortisol, ethanol, endorphin, Glucose, minerals, amino acids, vitamins, toxins, and so on. We know that the chemical balance represents the environment that our cells live in, and the change in this chemical balance can influence the functioning of our cells and that including gene expression.

Besides, we know that the mindset influences the chemical balance in a direct way. Still, the mindset can also indirectly influence our chemical balance and that via the lifestyle factors because we know that the lifestyle also depends on mindset.

So, put this in your mind, your mindset, influence your chemical balance directly or indirectly, then your chemical balance regulates your gene expression and affects every dimension of

---

[1] *Céline Tiffon; The Impact of Nutrition and Environmental Epigenetics on Human Health and Disease; International Journal of Molecular Sciences; 2018, 19, 3425.*

your life positively or negatively.

If we take as an example the stressful lifestyle, in other words, the habit of feeling stressed continually in life:
a study about the impact of stress on our DNA demonstrated that stress affects the telomeres[1], which are the physical ends of chromosomes that protect the DNA inside from damage. So that the longer the telomeres are, the more DNA is protected, and the shorter the telomeres are, the more the DNA becomes exposed to damage, which leads to countless health problems and premature aging.

In this study, the comparison of the relative lengths of telomeres in identical twins, who start life with similar genes, showed that emotional stress could result in one twin having a cellular age that is as much as ten years older by age 40, which means that having a stressful lifestyle can make you biologically older by 25% compared to your real age.

And knowing that stress is the most prevalent emotion in our epoch and distinguishes the lifestyle of hundreds of millions of people on this planet, stress becomes a real health problem in our epoch.

When I talk about the stress, I have to mention also gratitude[2], which I considered as the antidote to stress.

The gratitude is a positive emotion generated by a favorable chemical balance characterized by a high level of dopamine and

---

[1] *Your DNA is not your destiny: Behavioral epigenetics and the role of emotions in health; Anti-aging therapeutics; Vol. 13, pp. 35–42; 2010.*

[2] *Ahmad Valikhani, et al; The relationship between dispositional gratitude and quality of life: The mediating role of perceived stress and mental health; Personality and Individual Differences 141 (2019) 40–46.*

serotonin. This chemical balance can alter our biology, repair the damages caused by stress, and magnificently improve the quality of our lives and well-being. In other words, positive emotions can make positive epigenetic modulations.

So, put this in your mind; you can influence the expression of your genes purposely and positively in order to enhance your life and exploit your potential and that by adopting a positive mindset and positive emotional state.

THE TENTH PRINCIPLE

The same level of energy drives the same quality of life

The emotional states reflect the quality and the quantity of the triggered chemicals in our brains and bodies that affect the work of every cell in our brains and bodies, and that including energy production. The favorable chemical balance supports the proper functioning of our brains and bodies, which produce positive energy that make us better placed to attain what we aim. Unfortunately, the unfavorable chemical balance provides negative energy that prevents us from achieving what we want. Besides, the mindset and the chemical balance influence the electromagnetic field of the body (generate mainly by the heart and brain) and the vibrations that we send around us (the signals we send to the world). So, to produce changes in our lives, we must produce a variation in our energy; this means, when we change our level of energy, we change the quality of our life.

NB: The level and the quality of energy can be an indicator of the quality of chemical balance.

The chemical balance affects the production of the adenosine triphosphate or ATP in our cells, knowing that the ATP is the essential energy currency of all living organisms, including the human being.

Besides, the mindset and the chemical balance influence the electromagnetic field of the body, which is generated mainly by the heart and brain; also, the mindset and the chemical balance influence the vibrations that we send around us, which are the signals we send to the world.

The heart is the most powerful source of electromagnetic energy in the human body, producing the largest rhythmic electromagnetic field comparing to the other body's organs.

The chemical balance that is translated into negative emotions influences the functioning of the heart and the energy that it sends as vibrations. Where negative chemical balance gives negative vibrations, and positive chemical balance gives positive vibrations.

So, put this in your mind; your chemical balance significantly affects your energy.

The chemical balance that accompanies the moments of negative emotions such as boredom, emptiness, confusion, doubt, disappointment, lack of self-confidence, and lack of self-esteem, produces negative energy that I call it the lower negative energy or the energy of sabotage. This kind of energy drives us to abandon what we want to achieve irrationally. So, the energy of sabotage marks the beginning of self-destruction.

Besides, the negative energy that characterizes the moments of negative emotions like acute stress and anger can be very harmful; this energy I call it the massive destructive energy. The massive destructive energy often causes big mistakes and irreparable damage such as the end of a relationship, a serious health problem, tragic violence, missing great opportunities, losing time and money, and so.

However, the chemical balance that accompanies the moments of positive and powerful emotions such as love, enthusiasm, passion, and burning desire, is able to engender great positive energy that I call it the higher positive energy or the big feats' energy; this latter leads to fabulous accomplishments in our world. This kind of energy is the best to move to action because they allow us to overcome obstacles, to excel, to move forward despite all challenges, to go beyond our limits, to change, to grow, to rebound, to finish up a big task, to persevere, and to reach the most extraordinary dreams.

Besides, the positive energy that characterizes the moments of positive emotions like peacefulness, respect, admiration, relaxation, gratitude, appreciation, recognition, and fullness is very helpful energy. This energy, I call it the primary positive energy or the equilibrium energy. It is the energy of knowledge, recovery, and reconstruction. It is the best energy to make strategies and feedbacks, make big decisions, set goals, make resolutions, and so on.

So, put this in your mind; your energy indicates the quality of your life.

THE ELEVENTH PRINCIPLE

Consciousness defines reality

We have an infinite number of possible realities for ourselves that exist in this world at the same time until we observe them where the consciousness level of each one of us obliges us to pick one possibility at a time to become our single personal reality. When we change our way of thinking and broaden our consciousness, we can take other possibilities, perceive further options, seize new opportunities, and improve our lives, which leads us to make a completely different reality and entirely different experiences. The level of awareness of each person defines his /her reality, and the change in this level, unable him/her from shifting to another reality. In other words, the reality that we are living now is just one possible way of living from an infinite number of possibilities that were all existing at the same time until our consciousness interfered and chose one possible reality. Actually, we are the leader of our lives, and we have the possibility to orientate it as we want by changing our level of consciousness. So, when we change our mindset and broaden our consciousness, we can improve our lives and take other possibilities. That leads us to make a completely different reality and an entirely different experience.

One of the most remarkable experiences in quantum physics is the double-slit experience. In a very simple way, this experience concludes that when we send a small particle through a double slit, and we observe this experience simultaneously, we find that the small particle traverses the double slit as an object and gives an expected pattern on the screen. However, when we send a particle, and we don't observe how this particle will be traversing through the double slit, the result is astonishing. Without observing the experience, the pattern on the screen demonstrates that the particle was crossing both slits at the same time and was moving like a wave of possibilities meaning this particle can be everywhere at the same time. That means the particle goes through all the possible paths simultaneously, which form a wave of probability where all the possibilities are layered on each other.

In the simplest form, with observation, the particle behaves like an object and takes only one possible way. But without observation, this particle behaves like a wave where all the possibilities exist at the same time.

The observation is the measurement materials and the researchers' minds that represent the consciousness. This means that it is the consciousness that decides the positions of the particle and defines its reality. When we generalize this quantum phenomenon, we find that we always have an infinite number of possibilities in our lives. However, the intervention of our consciousness drives us to take just one possibility at a time.

Consciousness is predominantly defined by your mindset, which means that your mindset defines your reality.

Therefore, when you start making attention that you always have an infinite number of possibilities to live in your existence and that your mindset is creating your actual life, you begin to recognize that you are the leader of your life, and you can orientate it as you want.

THE TWELFTH PRINCIPLE

The new desired situation becomes a reality when it is incarnated

The wanted change becomes a reality when we completely embody it mentally, emotionally, and physically. Mentally means adapting our mindset according to the wanted change by changing our way of thinking, adopting new beliefs, and modifying our automatic programs to fit with what we want. Emotionally means to have feelings and emotions in coherence with what we want as change, which refers to have a favorable chemical balance in the brain and body. Physically means adjusting our actions and behaviors with the wanted change.

Doing or practicing is the best way to learn new skills, change our lives, and create a better reality. When we practice and experience new things such as a new desired situation, we are able to produce lasting changes in our minds, brains, and bodies that make the desired new situation becomes a living reality. So, we have to incarnate the new desired life mentally, emotionally, and physically in order to make it manifest tangibly.

The majority of people on this planet are born, live, and die without discovering their true potential and their real abilities; they spend their whole existence living lives don't belong to them. They adopt a limited mindset and a negative emotional state that makes them stay far away from their real capacities.

The real change in life begins when you start using your real potential, and that is only possible when you maintain your emotional state and your mindset in coherence with the wanted change until it becomes an integrative part of your reality.

So, if you want to unleash your true potential, you have to incarnate what you wish to mentally, emotionally, and physically.

And, put this in your mind, when you have the right mindset and the right emotional state, the impossible becomes possible, the unachievable becomes achievable, the unrealizable becomes realizable, and the most extraordinary dreams become a reality.

NB: we can even fake it until we make it.

A new life is waiting outside the comfort zone.
Create a life in your mind

THE LIFE DOMAINS ACCORDING TO THE SNCA APPROACH

The equilibrated life is based on a positive mindset that translated to a positive emotional state that refers to favorable chemical balance in the brain and body. Therefore, to have a great life full of happiness and satisfaction, we need to pay attention to our chemical balance and especially the main four chemicals for a positive and satisfying life which they are: serotonin, endorphin, dopamine, and oxytocin. So, according to these four chemicals, the SNCA approach divides the life departments into four departments or sides in our lives:

I. The Philosophy of Life

This department is the most important one because it impacts directly and profoundly the other departments of life.

Life philosophy includes convictions, believes, expectations, the meaning of life, meaning of things, perceptions, viewpoints, values, and spirituality. The positive life philosophy is related to favorable chemical balance and especially to a high level of serotonin and dopamine, which refers to some helpful emotions like gratitude, appreciation, satisfaction, and serenity. Unfortunately, the negative life philosophy is related to unfavorable chemical balance and especially a high level of cortisol for an extended period of time, which refers to some bad emotions like long-term stress, anxiety, and depression.

II. The Physical Dynamicity

This department is essential for our health and wellbeing also for regulating the chemical balance.

The physical dynamicity includes movements, work tasks, pleasant activities, body attitude, practicing sport, physical engagement, and any spent physical efforts. Physical dynamicity is essential for the excellent functioning of the brain and body; also, it promotes health and wellbeing. Physical efforts are extremely important for regulating our chemical balance, and particularly it permits to liberate the endorphin and reduce the cortisol, which refers to a good change in the emotional state and the adoption of a favorable chemical balance.

III. The Accomplishments

This department is the most known one and represents the growth in life.

Accomplishments include goals achievement, mission accomplishment, vision realizations, learn new skills, win some things, intellectual progress, financial improvement, professional advancement, and merely getting something done or practicing a passion. Accomplishments are essential for having a balanced life because the growth, progress, and amelioration in life is nature in the human being. Also, accomplishments have a significant impact on the chemical balance, especially decreasing the level of cortisol and liberating dopamine, which refers to good changes in the feelings and emotions.

IV. Social Bonding

This department represents the contact with the other people.

Social bonding includes having friends, having partner, spending convivial moments, collective activities participation, contributions to society, contact with family members, relationships with colleagues, helping people, and so on. The social bonding is excellent for the emotional state regulation because having a good relationship with the people full of respect, consideration, empathy, and love permits to have a favorable chemical balance, especially the release of oxytocin that supports the well functioning of the brain and body which allows feeling love, being passionate and persisting in this life.

THE MAIN REQUIREMENTS FOR DURABLE CHANGE "SNCA APPROACH"

In the simplest form, there are three main requirements for any durable and positive change according to the SNCA approach to positive change:

1- Define the new desired situation:

The identification of what you want precisely is crucial for any possible change. Having a direction in your life and knowing what you want is the first step to change it because ones the desired situation is defined and the new positive image is created in your mind, new neurological, chemical, and biological changes start to emerge in your brain and body, which prepare the tangible manifestation of what you want in your reality.

So, knowing what you want is crucial to unleash your potential and make a positive change in your life, and the best way to do that properly is by setting goals.

Here is a simple method that can help to clarify what you want the most in your life:

This method I call it the comparison method.

It is about identifying what matters the most to you by positioning yourself in different situations throughout your life. We can summarize this method in the following steps:

- Choose a quiet place, and be sure not to be disturbed for a while, and ask yourself the following question: What are the things that I really would achieve in life? Then list all the answers on a sheet of paper.

- Imagine yourself in the last minutes of your life, and ask yourself this question: what am I regretting the most about not having realized in my life? Then list all the answers on a sheet of paper.

- Imagine that you could go back in time and relive your whole life, and ask yourself this question: how could I relive my life and what would I want to do, have, and be? Then list all the answers on a sheet of paper.

- Imagine that you now have the power to realize anything in the blink of an eye, and ask yourself: what are the things you want to add to your life now? Then list all the answers on a sheet paper.

- Finally, take the four sheets and highlight the repeated answers. Then ask yourself this question: if I could only do one thing, which one would I choose? The answer will be the primary goal of your life.

Here is another simple method that can make clearer what you want in a specific period of time:

- Please write down the most important things you want to accomplish in a specific period of time (for example, I want to accomplish this thing in one month, six months, one year, and so on).

- Ask yourself the following question: if I could immediately realize only one thing from this list using, for example, a magic wand, what thing could bring the most significant improvement in my life? The answer to this question represents your main goal for the duration that you have defined.

2- *Adjust the mindset to fit with the new desired situation*:

It is fundamental to modify your way of thinking, regulate the automatic programs, and adapt your beliefs to fit with the desired situation. Once it is done, real chemical and neurobiological modifications occur in the brain and body in coherence with what you want, which makes the change becomes natural, habitual, spontaneous, and logical for you.

The twelve principals of the SNCA approach that you have learned during this course are already changed many beliefs in your mind and already provided you much empowering information that shaped your mindset in a positive way. Now, maintaining a positive and powerful inner dialogue helps a lot to have a positive and lasting mindset. The powerful inner dialogue that can unleash your true potential and help you make a positive change must turn around the possibility, the capability, and the deservedness. Which means what you want to achieve is possible and achievable. Also, you are personally capable of achieving what you want. As well, you deserve to achieve what you want and to have a better life.

It is possible to do it

You are capable of doing it

You deserve it

However, to reveal more information about the nature of your inner dialogue, you need to ask yourself some questions such as:

Is this self-talk making me feel good or bad?

Is it helping me to make a positive change or not?

Is it making me progress in my life or holding me back?

Is it helping me to make a positive change or not?

Is it serving the achievement of my goals or not?

Is it helping me to preserve a favorable chemical balance or not?

Is it serving me to be healthier or not?

Is it helping me to build positive habits or bad ones?

Is it helping me to reprogram my subconscious mind positively or negatively?

Here are some examples of positive and powerful inner dialogue expressions:

I am ready to have a better experience.

I deserve to achieve such a great goal.

I am confident and certain that I can do it.

I have all that is necessary to begin realizing what I want.

I am sure that I can turn my dream into reality.

I am always up to my challenges.

I am the only one responsible for the direction of my life.

Everything I can think about and believe in, I am able to realize.

Every day I am more and more motivated to achieve my dream.

I am excited to wake up every day and take a few steps towards my goal.

I have a burning desire to fulfill my dream.

I feel more and more grateful in my life.

I control my life, and I will make it exceptional.

I am bigger than any challenge I encounter.

I learn and grow through every experience.

I am ready to start living a different life.

I am ready to unleash my true potential.

I deserve a new and better existence.

Life is beautiful.

3- *Live the desired situation*:

When you practice what you want to be, you accelerate the neurobiological and the chemical modifications pace. So, persist and repeat until these neurobiological and chemical modifications become lasting, which means repeat until the new desired situation becomes an integral part of your life.

You can be the most brilliant mind in this plant, but without involving yourself in what you want, nothing will happen.

Once you clearly define what you want, and you adopt a positive mindset that fits with it, the big part of the job is done, but it needs to be finalized by feeling, behaving, and acting according to it.

Practicing visualization can help you to develop a strong feeling about what you want, which allows taking actions that lead to getting what you want rapidly.

Here is a short exercise that can help to have a great day :

Choose a quiet place in the morning before starting your day.

Keep a slow and deep breath.

Imagine the perfect and accelerated scenario of your day, and then imagine the positive feelings and emotions, such as self-confidence, self-esteem, satisfaction, and gratitude that gradually increase as time flies, regardless of the situations you would meet during your day.

Imagine yourself doing what you need to do on this day in order to move a step forward to your dream.

Imagine yourself overcoming the daily challenges with intelligence, serenity, and efficiency.

Feel every detail intensely and make this powerful image last as long as possible.

Repeat this exercise every morning. Also, you can do it as the last task of the day before.

After a certain time, the created positive image will positively reprogram your subconscious mind, which helps you to achieve what you want.

Through this short book about the SNCA approach, we have seen powerful and fascinating information that will help you significantly to improve the quality of your life. So at the end of this book, I have nothing left but to wish you all the best. Good luck and remember

Give a direction to your life,

Live with positive thoughts,

Live with powerful beliefs,

Live with positive habits,

Live with positive emotions,

Live with positive expectations,

Live with hope,

Live with gratitude,

Live with love,

Live with an open mind to new beliefs and possibilities,

Unfold your great dreams mentally, emotionally, physically

And enjoy your life.

To change your reality, you have to design a new one in your mind, and stick on it mentally and emotionally until it overcomes the unwanted reality.

Khaled BOUKEBBOUS

THE AUTHOR

Khaled Boukebbous is a scientist passionate about the mind-body connection and the mind-reality interaction. He is the founder of the new approach that we have talking about in this book, "sustainable neurochemical alteration - SNCA." Additionally, he is the founder of positive minds impact.

Dépôt légale: Octobre 2020